T0157275

Secret Chambers of The Heart

Deborah Boone

authorHOUSE®

AuthorHouse™
1663 Liberty Drive
Bloomington, IN 47403
www.authorhouse.com
Phone: 1 (800) 839-8640

Published by AuthorHouse   10/05/2018

ISBN: 978-1-4685-0129-2 (sc)
ISBN: 978-1-4685-0128-5 (e)

Library of Congress Control Number: 2017911265

Print information available on the last page.

Any people depicted in stock imagery provided by Thinkstock are models, and such images are being used for illustrative purposes only. Certain stock imagery © Thinkstock.

This book is printed on acid-free paper.

Dedication

To My Most Adorable Husband

I take this opportunity to show my gratitude in heart for the many prayers you've prayed for such, great sacrifices of your time, energy, and love. For your faithfulness and relentlessness to hold fast and stay with me through all my hardships and many struggles.

For being my comforter and my best friend. For your much needed support and words of wisdom

I take this time and this great opportunity to acknowledge you for without you the gift God has given me to write by and through His anointing and the wonderful treasure of your awesome love it would not have been possible to write much of this book.

It is to the glory of God that secrets of my heart and the riches of His treasure chest is poured out through my writings.

You are my inspiration and the intrigue part of my soul. It is your love that has truly inspired such a beauty of a rose to open up and flourish. I love you with all my heart.

Signed;

The love of your life
Your wife

In Acknowledgment of:

My Eldest Daughter

Debra Holstead and my friend Norma Pearson for they're faithfulness in supporting me with encouragement and much prayers. For the support needed at a difficult time.

I thank you and honor you for being there for me.

To All My Readers

I've been blessed and chosen to be a writer for God

To express his beauty for today and tomorrow.

Its the privilege given to me to help erase someone's sorrow and misery;

He's poured into me if you'll just read

A world of beauty that I've traveled through in tests and trials when I felt Oh so blue

As you read this book I pray you'll discover too,

The beauty of suffering that has poured out love through God's great instructions

My private thoughts I do share from my heart –

While whispering a prayer. I know they too will impart to your heart

The glory of God's beauty.

A Book of Inspirations
May You Truly Be Inspired

Contents

Part II
Songs In The Night

Part III
"A Mother's Heart"

Part IV
"The Winner In You"!

Part V
Creating My World

Part I
"A Light in My Heart"

"Thy Kingdom Come"

One night I sat and thought of all my troubles

I could see no way out. My future was so very dim

I cried, I prayed, sometimes at night I was wide eyed awake. After

so long of a time toiling through many days and nights of severe

anguish in heart and mind I found the strength to just get up again

I found the courage to say I can win

I discovered a faith much deeper began to rise from within

And suddenly I believed I could be free of this thing

I praised, I worshipped my way through

I believed in Him and in the end I did win.

Yes, He freed me from within His Kingdom had come

And now God's will in me was done

as it was planned, defined, by God's hand for my life

Thy Kingdom came down to earth.

His will was done

Finally I had won.

To God be the Glory
Written by the inspiration of the Holy Spirit

"M Best Friend"

I went for a walk this morning, my feet took me
on a path that lead to visit my best friend and O'
what a welcome surprise did I find within.

As the door opened He bid me to come in

I said to My Best Friend, good morning Dear Jesus,
How are you on this morning? How do you feel?
What do you desire that I should do for you?

As I bowed in heart at my Saviours feet, I felt
the longing in my heart to just be
me and be free to express all my heart

As I repeated the question to my friend I sat very quietly
and sought to be still. Suddenly I discovered such a
welcome surprise, Jesus and me sat O' so High. High above
all powers and principalities. We sat seated together in
heavenly places and O the glory that filled this place

As we sat on a cloud way up high above the earth,
I could feel no care of this Old world.

My heart was made open for my Saviour to see
the care, the warmth of my visit with Him.

As I drew near to see how He was doing
on this bright cheerful morning,

I wanted Him to know most how dear to me He is.
His friendship is precious to me.

I sat on the cloud and laid my head on His shoulder. He put
His arm around me as the cloud carried us away into a secret
place. It was my friend's quiet place. Just Jesus and me.

"M Best Friend" *(continued)*

The view was breathtakingly beautiful. You see up so high
way up in the sky, I could see with my eyes, the east, the west,
the north, the south. Nothing was in view but the sky opened
with such a pretty blue. Just openness all around as far as the
eye could see, and there on the cloud sat Jesus with me.

My heart was delighted at being so privileged.
Just think, my King sat listening to His friend and
enjoying every moment, hearing my secrets.

Do you know how wonderful I felt? I said to my friend, Jesus
I know why John the beloved loved you so, I understand why
he had to sit so close and lay his head on your bosom the
most. He'd chosen other disciples yet He loved John most.

I felt like John oh so close. I embraced this place
of solitude and basked in the moment

I felt the Lord is my shepherd I shall not want
that 23rd psalm came to my mind.

There was quietness all around. His love was crystal clear and in
the nearness of that moment in time, solitude flooded with cheer

My whole being was in oneness with Jesus. It was a perfect peaceful
place of rest. Just setting there laying my head on His breast.

If you could see so way up high far above the earth, there is
a picturesque view of open sky with such a perfect view. The
blanket floor covered the earth below, and that which was above
was more in store of the vastness of the beauty the skies laid
scrolled. Such a peaceful place of happiness. I was His guest and
yes, I was blessed to be privileged by God to enjoy today's best.

My best friend, my best place, my best rest.

I just had to come see how you are on today, to tell you how
wonderful and precious you are. I care about how you feel. I just
want you to know how really I feel. You are so dear, dear, dear

I love you Lord but you love me best. I'm privileged
to know you its only through each test.

To God be the glory for all the beauty I see in me.
The work of art He created me to be.

"Gifted To Love"

Gifted to love by my Saviour shed blood

O What a cost what a price paid for my loss

I have no excuse that I can use for Romans 2:1 says - old inexcusable man you're without an excuse who hath bewitched you that you should not obey the gospel of truth.

I have a purpose for my majestic birth

It is to help save souls from a burning hell here below.

Now that I'm gold and its bee made known my purpose for my birth

How do I go fishing for these precious lost souls.

It is written follow me (Jesus) and I will make you fishers of men. Be like Jesus. Act like Jesus.

Amen!

"Jesus Paid The Cost"

Jesus Paid the cost to set all men free from sin

You ask what exactly are my sins

Sin is all things that are against the will of God

Sin is all things done by and through your
body that's harmful to your nature

Sin is even disobedience to the law of His written Holy Word
that shows us and tells us what is right and wrong

It tells us how to keep from paying a great
cost for going alone on your own

It says if we follow after the desires of our own flesh

There's a great penalty and you'll be the
guest for the rest of your lives

In hell you'll left up your eyes because of your mess

But God has prepared a rest and offers you His best

Yes, a table is spread and the feast of The Lord Is Ready!

He'll share to all who heeds His call

He's a loving God who died for us all

So my friend take this good news within and open the door
of your heart and Jesus will free you from the sin within

He'll forgive no matter how great the sin (wrong)

"Jesus Paid The Cost" *(continued)*

He loves you best and wants in the end that you should win.

A golden crown of eternal life is laid up for all who win over sin

In the end His promise you'll see life eternal
because you dare to come in

Into His Kingdom above the heavens He has
prepared to reign with you forever

You'll walk the streets of gold because of a new immortal soul

You'll live a life all dressed in white

An overcomer you have chosen to be

Jesus will say well done you've gained the victory

So my fellow brethren and friends

Jesus is beckoning to you won't you please let him in

He wants to come into your heart. Change
your life for He has paid the cost

Yes! He died upon the cross. His blood came
streaming down to the ground

Will you be free says He from this old world of sin

For I shed my blood to wash away your sins and
free you from within every debt you owe has been
paid. He became the price of your sin

Jesus loves you so and He wants you to know

You can gain life eternal if you'll only let Him in

So open up the door. Will you choose Him today and be
made free from all sin? or pay the cost and die lost?

Written from the heart of God
especially to you!
To God be the glory

Deborah Boone

"Secret Chambers of My Heart"

There's a beauty so rare that the naked eyes can't always see

This beauty is only found in the eyes of the beholder.

You see this beauty is hidden very deeply within the soul.

It takes a very special love for it to unfold

Not all eyes can behold because some would say its imperfect,
others would be jealous and still others the critics at large

But there is a masterpiece of every believer

Its a new heart, its pure and its taught by God to depart from
anything and all things that would contaminate and spoil

It's sought out by God it's brought through His
shed blood and its priceless in His sight

You see it is the righteousness of God. It's offered
to all but only a few will heed to His call

He ever beacons to sinners near and far even to those who
profess they've accepted His call, but refuse to change

Refuse to conform to His will and His ways

They are what we call self-righteous because they obey not His laws

There is a book of deeds kept in heaven, it has writings, confessions
of everything you've ever said or done whether, right or wrong.

From start to finish from the day newborn you arrived home

"Secret Chambers of My Heart" *(continued)*

Till the end of your funeral sending
you to your designated home

Whatever your choose whether right or wrong you
have the choice to choose your eternal home.

One day you will stand before His throne, judgment will be given
and He'll be able to say to you welcome home a job well done

Not every one is qualified to enter in

You must begin by saying Jesus please come in heed my cry
for I've lived in sin and I must needs to be born again

Born of your spirit so I can depart from sin
and be washed in your blood

Made brand new again redeemed from a world of prideful sins.

Now I am blessed, I took Jesus and I can
rest, In Him I can live life's best

And in the end I will gain eternal rest

I'll sit at my saviors feet and be blessed.

Deborah Boone

"No Secret"

There is no secret what God can do

He'll do for others like he'll do for you

I have an illness that people don't quite understand

But I know Jesus is still holding my hand

Some days it's hard to cope and on occasion I have fallen into a slope

The ups and downs, the ins and outs

But Jesus knows I'll soon come around

I don't care what people might say, I go on anyway

Even when the sun don't shine I let it shine in this heart of mine

Lit it shine, Let it shine, Let it shine just one day at a time

Jean Donald

"God's Hand"

God keeps me from hurt, harm, and danger,

He shields and protects me when sometimes I
don't know whether I'm right or wrong. He has His
hands over me so that nothing can go wrong

He protects me when I am sleeping when
I know it won't be any weeping

When I go to and from, I know God is looking here below

When I am hungry and need something to eat

He provides and supplies all my needs
When I am worried or upset, God is there saying do not fret

My mind goes up and down But God knows that I will come around

God's got His hands on me that's why I am so pleased

By Jean Donald

My daughter suffered from an illness called
schizophrenia. She wrote this to encourage those who
suffer from any mental or emotional challenges.

"It Is Finished"

Prophesy to these mountains and declare
my God doeth great exploits

Speak unto these rocks and cause them to tremble

Tell these walls you must come down

For my God who is mightier He rules, He reigns over all

Declare unto the earthly realm His power I do proclaim

For God is not a man that He should lie

Once, twice, thrice, has it been told

The God of all has all power in His Hand and
He reigns, He reigns, He reigns

At the name of Jesus every knee must bow

All things in heaven, all things upon earth every
creature even below, at the sound of His voice

How great, How mighty How powerful the sound of His voice.

It clashes upon the waters and causes a great roar

He speaks from the heavens and the sound
of thunder is heard upon earth

One disciple of Old declared His voice is as many waters

who can stand before Him

What valley is so low that His

"It Is Finished" (continued)

power can not exalt it

What river in your life seems so uncrossable He can't bring you over?

Is there a night so dark He can't see you through?

No! no night so dark can conquer you when God is on your side

His strength is made perfect in weakness.

Our God reigns. He rules He made the heavens
and the earth and the fullness thereof

Trust and obey believe what He says you will be the proof of
His word that stands unafraid to prove in the test of time

Jesus never fails

It is finished, it is finished

Every mountain has been removed

Every valley is exalted

Every bondage He has broken

Every fetter has been removed

Every chain no longer visible

Every wall has fallen down to the ground

Every darkness He has turned to light

All the ashes are now beauty

The garment now arranged in His glory

And people shall hear of His amazing story
and behold all of His glory

For He has crowned me with glory and honor

Favor His hand held out to me

Favor with man and favor with God

Power with God and power with man

"It Is Finished" *(continued)*

Even the hills are made low

For by God's power

I've triumphed over every foe

What once was unbeatable has been stomped to the ground
under my feet have I crushed the backs of my enemies

I pursued in the name of Jesus and in His strength did I draw from

I took His word and lassoed in His truth, faith
that came on board and victory was in view

I talked it, I worked it This word He gave

His instructions I obeyed. Now, I know whatever the battle

His word once proclaim gives way to
victory and gain again and again

I proclaim by the power of God It is truly
finished and my God doth reign

"Overflow Is Here"

I wondered through a wilderness

A long, hard, and tedious journey

At times I felt so all alone but these were only my
feelings that dealt with the facts of life

Truth was invisible blinded by circumstances

I thought I had prayed and prayed until there
were no more prayers I could pray

A day came when so many years of hardship had gone
by and on this day my faith of confession I did cry

I declared I was no longer to live restricted

I decreed I've had it and have a breakout in every area of my life

That satan had tried to confine me and deny me the right
to be free and enjoy the liberty Christ paid for me

My soul had sat so quiet within

Yet Jesus understood my silence was not sin

A hunger and thirst for life to just live
was crying out so deep within

I yearned to be free from this long laborious journey

Yet I knew it was working together for my good

"Overflow Is Here" *(continued)*

I knew the Master repeatedly said to me

There's another side that you can't see

It's more to it than meets the eye

The sun will shine and the best is yet to come
and there are brighter days ahead

He spoke and said, its not designed to kill you, you'll live and not die

You can make it and by the power of God you
will prosper in the name of Jesus

I wanted out so badly until

Jesus was moved with compassion He had mercy and grace
upon me. He taught me a more powerful way to pray

These are words that flowed from the depths of my soul

Not rhyming, not poetic, all together, but yet
poetry that poured out of my heart

It was a cry, a plea yet sweet as wine and full of hope for life

He said unto me take unto thee the prophesies I've
spoken to thee and pray them as prayers

Just speak my word and it shall be unto thee
a bridge to cross over on them

So, I took His words, His spoken promises
and into my mouth I spoke them out

And they did go forth as a seed planted into the ground

Watered by faith through His amazing grace

He said the more often you'll proclaim it the more you
will see the words of promise I have given to thee

Just freely speak and the giants before you shall fall to the ground,
they'll even perish at the resounding of what you'll sound out for in
it is life I'll cause it to be, even I shall quicken it and hasten it to be

So I put His Rhema into my mouth

"Overflow Is Here" *(continued)*

Diligently I prayed both day and night often for days without end

Now, I know that faith is the substance of things
hoped for and the evidence of things not seen

So I spoke these words professing and confessing them unto my King

My soul yearned to just be free

No longer wearied of my life, I received the
overflow Jesus reserved for me

Deborah Boone

"God's Way Out!"

Prophets and intercessors God is calling to you

From the east, to the west, from the north to the south

Come! Come! Come! saith He

Prophesy and intercede there is a need

To heed the voice of God and receive His plead

He is beckoning to one and all to enter His call

He's crying, He's proclaiming to the nations I'll send thee

Come teachers, Come preachers, evangelists too,

My fields are white my harvest is ripe

tell the people its time to prepare and get it right

My trumpet will sound and Gabriel will blow

The goodness to every ready soul,

Don't be lost, don't be tossed

Don't be deceived God's way is the only remedy

Jesus did pay

To save the soul from hell and yet a greater debt to be paid

Eternal life in a lake of fire was never designed by God for mankind

It was for satan and His evil angels

"God's Way Out!" *(continued)*

Whom God did band from the gates of heaven

Choose ye this day whom you will serve

Your price He has already paid for the sins
of the nations that has raged

Babies are dying because mother's are crying
abort, abort, this is my choice

Prophets and preachers, great men and women are the
masterpieces of God's creation and decision –

To be carried in the womb of many women

Die, Die, that is my choice, but on judgment day you'll hear its cry

You'll have to tell Jesus why O' why?

Repent of your evil, abstain from your wicked way

Unless you've become a victim innocent to the crime

You'll have a great price to pay

The pleasure of your flesh only last but for a moment

Sin condemns and in the end who will win?

God is calling O' earth unto the far ends

He's crying in the highways and byways too

He's searching through the fields for you and you

He wants to pardon you

He says: I've given you my best

He stood the test – Jesus

paid the price so you could rest –

Cease from your labor, toil no more, lay your sins down at Jesus door

Exchange it today for an immortal soul

Deborah Boone

"God's Way Out!" *(continued)*

How? Just ask Jesus to come into your heart, Cleanse
me from all my sins and it will depart

I know I've done wrong, forgive me I pray

Grant me today in my heart come and stay

Lord, I'm willing, I will obey,

Thy word will I hide in my heart so I shall not stray

Thy precepts I will keep to enlighten me on my way

I'll take heed to my way to please thee in all I do and say

Lord, please come into my heart,

And just show me thy way

Teach me to pray thy

Kingdom come thy will be done –

As it is in heaven on earth so let it be

Lord Jesus I accept thee as my King

To rule and reign over me in all things

That I may be with thee throughout E-tern-i ty.

Lord, teach me to live

Holy, daily with thee.

Together

```
T O G E     T H      E R
e t r n     r o      v e
a h e d     i w (to) e a
c e a u     a        r c
h r t r(in) l           h (up higher)
i s a s
n n
g c
  e
```

Deborah Boone

Push

P	U	S	H
r	n	o	a
a	t	m	p
y	i	e	p
	l	t	e
	h	n	
	i	s	
	n		
	g		

Joy

You can win in the heat of the battle with

J	O		Y
e 1st	t		o
s	h		u (Last)
u	e (second)		
s	r		
	s		

Food for Thought
Temperance:

Temperance means more than just being abstinent. It is having the ability and courage to have self control anytime anyplace, anywhere

"The Passion of My Heart"

This is one I love dearly

He is the passion of my heart

He is the longing of my soul

He's the apple of my eye

He's the wind beneath my feet

He's the very breath I breathe.

He's the reason that I live but Oh what a reason

He's the beauty in my world that I live in

He's all that I could ever desire and need

He's the sweet fragrance of the beautiful aroma I wear

I'm complete in Him

When He wraps His arms of love about me I feel
safe, secure, and I rest upon His breast

He's my best friend

He's the love of my soul

Nothing and no one can separate our hearts

He's 1st and always at the forefront of my mind

He's always willing too oblige

He's thoughtful, He's caring

"The Passion of My Heart" *(continued)*

He's mindful at all times

He's gentle, He's strong,

He has a sense of humor all His own

He's powerful, He's holy, He's wonderful, someone I adore

He's a man who has passions and yet He is God

He has emotions like you and me

And if we'll take the time to listen

He will tell us what He feels and even what He sees

He has needs or didn't you know

His praises due Him are a delight to His soul

We were created for His pleasure that we might give Him glory.

He inhabits the praise of men

To God be the Glory
in all that I say and do

"The Wind of the Spirit"

The wind of the spirit is blowing in the heart of the earth

It's a fresh new wind that's urshering the power, glory
and authority of God greater than ever know

Its moving in the heart of the earth

In signs, wonders, and miracles

It proclaims God's authority that His coming is near

He wants us to grab hold to this great liberty

To all who dare to hear

That He's doing a new thing in the earth even in the atmosphere

He's sending signs and wonders throughout the earth

He's showing His glory so boldly

By touching the sick and making every one whole

Limbs are growing, His glory shinning boldly

Eyes are being restored missing in sockets

Arms you'll see stretch forth before the eyes

At the spoken word as He commands thee

Lame will walk, no more wheelchairs will they need

Cancers will fall before your feet

"The Wind of the Spirit" *(continued)*

Ears will grow where none appeared

Because the coming of the King draweth so near

Withered hands will stretch forth anew

As done in the days of old so its also new

Change souls will be saved, a new

wave of glory is on the way

You'll hear a revival take over the prisons

Men and women who can 't stop jibbering

About the power of God thats shaking the prisons

Drs. will be amazed at the sick in bed

Many declared mentally ill will be restored
and their illness will be no more

Yes! A new wave of glory is on the way bold
in Gods glory thats never been told

The wind of the spirit carried throughout the earth

Like the day of Pentecost cloven tongues will be set on fire again

Masses and masses of souls we must win

Tell them that Jesus return is coming (again)

Deborah Boone

"Lord, I Stand In Awe Of You"

For the beauty of the clouds the sky so bright white and blue

Lord I stand in awe of you when I see the sun that
declares the brightness of your glory

Lord, I stand In Awe of You.

The magnificence of the stars that captivates you

Lord I stand In Awe of You For the splendor of
the night that turns to morning light

Lord I stand In Awe of You

For flowers that bloom no man tends to,

For oceans that flow and all the beauty of this earth below

Lord, I stand In Awe of You when I behold all your colors so bold

Lord, I stand in awe of You

For the beauty of every season and the reason for change

Still I'm amazed by your beauty that never changes

Lord, how beautiful you are

Yes! I stand amazed

When I think of the wonder of your love

How you came from heaven above

Walked this earth below to give your life such a great sacrifice

"Lord, I Stand In Awe Of You" *(continued)*

To save a sinner like me

O' How I do stand so amazed

I'm amazed that this dust of the earth

You chose a lump of clay

Fashion and molded and gave

The right to be free and have life E-tern-a-ly

Lord, I stand amazed

when I see the human body

so creatively formed

and the beauty unlike any other

the unicorn

To hear the sound and distinguish the voice
in the different animals too

Lord, I truly do stand amazed at you

The trees, the mountains, streams that flow into the river

And yet it never overflows

Lord, I stand amazed at the beauty in you

To look and see the talents, the skills, the
creative ingenious you placed in man

To try to understand the origin of man

Lord, how awesome you are

Deborah Boone

"Lord, I Stand In Awe Of You" *(continued)*

I stand amazed at you

The body is formed all brand new

Each part woven intrigue from you.

Lord, what a wonder you are

I do stand amazed at you

This world you made just for man

Who had nothing to do with your plan

Is laid out by the master's own divine plan

Everywhere I look is beauty to see

Even the creative minds you've given to men

Who added to this world buildings still

And more and more did this world become a work of art

From God's own heart

Amazed Amazed am I

To see the faces so many very different but all mankind

Every race a different nation

What a wonder, what a mystery the mind of God

Who chose the wonder to be so kind as to
make many nations we call mankind.

Lord, I stand in awe of you!

"God's Best"

I gave my Lord the best of me

In my test, my trials, I was willing to surrender all of me

Sometimes my flesh got in the way caused me pain

I didn't want to pay

But I got on my knees and cried Lord, please hear my plea

I only want to give thee the very best of me

Satan was there, who tried to scare

All the faith, hope and confidence I had in me

But I dared to push pass and refused to die

I fought hard to keep hope alive

You see there were valleys so low at times

I wasn't sure if I could swim the tide

But, Jesus came along and on His wind I did ride

High above every scary tide

He was my shelter and in Him I did hide

Safely within even in the darkest of night

He took me on flight so I could soar way up high

"God's Best" *(continued)*

Like an eagle did I spread my wings

I soared high above many painful things.

Yes! I gave Jesus my best

You see by my writing I am blessed

For as you read you can see I stood my test(s)

I found favor in His sight

O my such a sweet delight

Never ever mumbled, grumbled or complained

You see I said Jesus I give you my best!

He said to me daughter of mine you touch me deeply down inside

Great favor and honor I bestow on thee because
you dared to give me the best of thee

"A Quiet Place"

There's a place I travelled to not so long ago

As a matter of fact it was a few days ago

It was a quiet place where I humbly bowed at my saviours feet

I entered into His throne room

There His presence made His abode

An invitation He did extend unto me

Welcome! He said come on in as I entered His throne room

I felt His presence a place I longed to be

We sat upon His throne and there attentively

He did listen to me

As my heart rejoiced over the love that flowed

from thoughts of gratitude and thanksgiving

No one knew the beauty that flowed from this
earthen clay a vessel He possessed

You see, I said, I've come to give you praise
for all the wonders I've beheld

I've come to give you praise for this another glorious day

As I knelt at His feet

"A Quiet Place" *(continued)*

I discovered a peace

a place of solitude

A hidden place where no one could enter but just my Saviour and me

It was quiet as I poured out my soul

He accepted the thanksgiving as my lips did render praise

And glory and honor to our most high

I smiled from deep down inside

You see its the place where one can come and rest

Its a place where you can give Him your best

A wondrous place that brings comfort and
ease to life struggles and test

Here in this place Jesus is willing to share His heart

He imparts His love to every heart

Broken, wounded, tattered, scorned, worn, makes no difference

His door is open and He welcomes you in love to just come on in

Silence was sweet and refreshing to my soul

As I poured out my love and worshipped Him

whom I adore

He inclined His ear His heart I felt with such cheer

He made me feel special

You see He loves me O' so dear

I felt a comfort that caused my soul to yield and as I sat still

I beheld the awesome

awakening of a closer walk with thee

A love welled up inside that brought tears too my eyes

"A Quiet Place" *(continued)*

That God would love me no matter what and somehow
someway it made me feel its just going to be okay!

I felt my soul crying out to thee

Lord come help me

I need you to fight for me

The more I prayed the greater I felt the praises

Deep down inside of me

It comforted my mind with His peace divine.

"Because He's God"

He can make the rough places smooth

He can cause the crooked to be made straight

He can cause water in desert places

He can make the wilderness to bloom

He can cause the mountains to bow down and be made lower

He can take the valley and exalt it this I know

He can cause the sun to shine in the darkest place

He can make a way when there is no way

He can cause the light to penetrate your night (darkest hour)

He can work a miracle right in the middle of your distress

He can take a mess and turn it, and make it blessed

He can turn your darkest hour to the brightest day

Yes! He can make a way out of no way

He takes the wrong and make it right

He can cause the devil to be put to flight

He can lift you up and turn you around

Cause the fear to turn like the noonday

He can make the sun to shine in this broken heart of mine

"Because He's God" *(continued)*

He can take the tears and wipe them away

Take one 24 hour and start life over I'll say!

Because He's God and God alone

He performs such great wonders

He can roll back the night and part fresh sunlight

And just because He's God

He causes us to triumph in such great victories.

Deborah Boone

"The Impossible Was"

I have a God who is a Great God

He is strong and mighty

He's powerful and that's not all

My God is able to do exceedingly, abundantly, above all

So prophesy, prophesy one and all

Our God rules, He reigns, He's higher above all

He's great in power, He's matchless in strength

He's a fortress, a shield and still

He's yet more than we comprehend, He has a divine will

The storms of life may blow and it may seem that there's no hope

Jesus takes control of the impossible that boast

In Him we can hope

He has the strength to keep us afloat

When the impossible boast and threatens all our hope

We can ride on through the tide

We have a captain on high

He's a watchman in the midnight seasons'

He knows how to guide us safely through

"The Impossible Was" *(continued)*

You see He has a purpose it's not just always our view

We have a matchless wonder

His voice roars and thunders

It causes our enemy to be scattered and run for cover

Yes! Mr. Impossible does boast loud and oh so strong

But though we know not we are safe on board
because the captain of our soul

is a watchman He's always on board

So to Mr. Impossible who tries to say so loud

Here this and know this

Jesus is always listening

He's the silent King who can do anything

He has His way in the storms of life

When the billows and the waves oh so heavily toss

Jesus speaks peace be still

He's our Heavenly Boss

He keeps us close for this

He died upon the cross

That He should have the right to have complete
control in each and everyones souls.

Yes! Mr. Impossible was because Jesus caught hold of him

Deborah Boone

"The Impossible Was" *(continued)*

He changed His name from Impossible to possible

Whatever your impossible situation may be there's hope
in Christ Jesus He's our saviour and His love is for real

He's able to speak to the impossible and say

Peace Be Still Amen!

"The Rainbow"

I am a promise of hope and expectation

I carry the joy of dreams and happiness to come

I am a dwelling place that you can run into

When storms of life come, I can cause you to maintain
your course by keeping your eyes upon me

When trials come and rob you of hope, I'm the
blessing that will help you stay afloat

When darkness seems to cover you round and about, and
you fret and despair because you see no way out

In the light that shines in the night I can revive you,
strengthen you and cause you to dream on

When satan brings His lies and says what can't be

I'm the promise of prophecy and if you'll look through my
eyes, you'll see all is bright and everything will be all right.

No matter the problem no matter the test

I'm the rainbow and I declare there's a rest

I'm a promise and I hold the best of everything
He's promised through your test

Remember this and don't forget I can cause you to
swim way out far until you reach your destiny

"The Rainbow" *(continued)*

Because I am a promise of hope my job is to keep you afloat

And to bring you into the blessed place of promise you've awaited

I'll journey with you as you keep me for your view

And in the end you'll see faithfully I have caused you to win

All your treasurers and blessing that was hidden til the end.

"The Garden"

There's a beauty side of God that is so wondrous, so
tender, so sweet, so easily touched and yet so Holy.

There's a wondrous side of God you can behold where He takes
on the role as a friend to peek inside the depth of your soul

There's a precious side of God where He takes the time
to spend with you and I. Its a secret place where Jesus
unveils all the glory and power and, majesty handed to
you, poured out of His heart to be treasured in yours.

There's yet so many other sides to God such a breath
taking view. He laughs and talks and shares with you.

He shows His rare side to only such a precious few because
others can see only the side of a Saviour from their view.

He is so High so lifted up He's majestic in all His ways and
pours out with out measure unto us His amazing grace

He sits and sups with us such a delight, such a
pleasure is He to spend His day with me

"The Garden" *(continued)*

He takes pleasure in His creation of man He has made liken
unto Him you see God inhabits the praise inside of each of us

Worthy Worthy Worthy is He

He rains on the just and the unjust to the saved He has
poured in His best, to the unsaved you are blessed.
For He daily loads us all with His benefits.

Did you know that the subconscious part of man is a part of God?

Its the part that says when you go to do wrong don't do
that or If I were you I wouldn't go there. It even warns of
things that will happen when we push past our limits.

Yes God has so intriquely woven us into His image
til we are blessed beyond our comprehension.

Part II
Songs In The Night

"My Most Precious Jewel"

I have a precious gift God has bestowed upon me

Its the rarest of all gems beautiful to see

Wondrous to behold a delight to anyone's
sight and its cheerful and bright

Its pure and white and if you'll look closely through into
it; you'll see its light penetrates the darkest darkness

Its unique in every way

It has many facets that's the least I can say.

When you hold it its soft and excitement fills your heart

You feel joy of such beauty rare

It has a scent all its own

it distinguishes itself so that none other can compare

It can at times produce different sounds because
of words spoken so sweet and dear

Sometimes it can chuckle it sees through my thoughts

Other times its masculine and strong it has a voice all its own.

Yet and still there are sounds unheard when
the thoughts are not so deeply heard

It smiles and it lights up like a Christmas tree

It plays music that's meant only to one so dear

"My Most Precious Jewel" (continued)

It has a shape and its amazing to see

It can bend and stretch stand tall and bold, it
can sit and it conforms to its mold.

It never goes beyond once the instructions are told

Yes, its designed by the hand of God It has
the very nature of a son of God

Its beautifully wrapped in tapestry of gold
and tied with a humble bow

I'm blessed beyond measure to receive this treasure

For my Father in heaven doth rarely ever

Give out such jewels as precious as he

He has the divine nature of God in him given to me

He's precious, He's different He's one of a kind

He's unique to say the least but He's mine all mine

My Precious Jewel

"My True Love"

My true love is a new kind of love. Its uncommon
and possesses a beauty rare

My true love is a gift from heaven above

Hand picked and chosen by God out of His very own treasure chest

What makes my true love so very different is
He is unique, one of a kind all its own

Ideally created in the mind of my heavenly Father above

Reached down through years of time and called all mine

Its divine in nature, pure and white its set
apart by Gods glorious light

And in His might He has sculptured and woven with His
delight a marriage that's right and so full of life

The charm you see as you look at me is the glory of God

His pride you see

The garments we wear as I do thee wed are
His handiwork being unveiled

My Heavenly Father takes pride in giving away this
bride to His proud son He honors with alms

I shall be one saith He be blessed for I
have fulfilled this my prophesy

I adorn you in white for purity in my sight

"My True Love" *(continued)*

I dress you in honor for this is my great delight
and as you unveil on your wedding night, I shower
you with my love for the rest of your life

There's Essence Rare to call your own a love we
will share none other has ever known

The beauty of the night fills all our senses with such sweet delight

God himself has laid out our robes upon our bed

His and Hers saith He to wear

Our chamber is filled with the sweet scent of heaven

There's the beauty of God's music sweetest notes ever heard and as
the splendor of the night unveils all the beauty of God 's gift to love

His (God's) heart finds pleasure in the two I thee do wed

Such beauty is too majestic to convey

Its His covenant given for those He alone doth wed.

To God Be the Glory
Written by Inspiration
of the Holy Ghost
By Deborah Boone

"The Longing Sound"

Something I had long for really yearned for

For it has been such a long, long, time

It was for the sound

The sound of my precious loves voice

Somewhere far away I knew one day I'd see him

But until that day would come I knew I needed Him

Time had long past by when His face I could see

Now there left a yearning for my soul to just be.........

Just have the moment of hearing His voice to
strengthen refresh and revive me.

How I longed to hear the sweet sound of his tender heart

His lips would impart such gentle words

I could feel in the distance His heart crying out to me
longing and waiting his time to share with me

How awesome it all appears to be

Its like a fog in the nite that covers all the beauty of the nite.

You await to see the dawning of the day for
you know the sun will bring new rays

And in that blissful moment of hope I await
my love my strength, my hope

"The Longing Sound" *(continued)*

The passion of my heart beating for thee

Pulling you closer and closer with every heartbeat

Suddenly, I hear the sound of your sweet voice

The moment awaited to long knowing you're so far

Yet I'm refreshed, revived and strengthened anew

For the sound of your voice has the comfort I knew

I hear the care, the concern in the tone of your voice

I feel the strength of your masculinity
reaching out to my gentle femininity

O' what a welcome surprise caught up in
this moment quite by surprise

I felt a loud thump at the door of my heart

It jarred and awakened me deep inside

I felt this loud thump again

I wanted him to hasten and come on in

Such beauty rare He possesses with care

His heart is all mine to share and as the days
and nights seem to drift and go by

Our eyes are on the clock watching and waiting for that majestic
moment when we will meet in that moment called time.

From the Divine
Guidance of the Holy Spirit
Too your heart from mine

Deborah Boone

"If I Could"

If I could just hear your voice what a great
joy it would bring to my heart

If I could feel your presence all my senses would come alive again

If I could just see your face and imagine the
look what a delight it would bring

If I could just be with you it would make all
the difference in this my world

If I could just have you to hug me just now at this
moment when I feel I need you the most

I know I would feel such comfort, that's
what I am in need of the most

In your arms I'm safe, I feel alive, strengthened,
revived a fresh and anew

In your arms yours and yours alone I've found such truth

Only if I could. If I could I'd love to shower you with my love
my words I've stored would pour out like rain if I could

If I could I would express as best I can what you
truly mean to me. Oh how I wish I could.

If I could I would tell you I now know the true meaning of
loneliness. You see deep inside of me is a place, that only you and
you alone live and I feel the emptiness but I'm still waiting

"If I Could" (continued)

If I could Oh I (how I long for you). I feel silent
tears because I hold you so very dear

If I could at this moment tell you how I need
you so, I feel so broken in my soul

If I could only see you such pain of I miss you would
quickly erase. My spirit would come alive and my healing
would take place just to see you face to face

In a blissful moment what a change would take place

Your love is more powerful than anything I've ever encountered.
It amazes me because it goes beyond the distance of time.

Whether near or far the truth be known every word
I've uttered is because of you and you alone.

I miss you more today than words can or will ever convey.

My heart is yours and yours alone. My heart
today is saying to you If only I could

I miss you so much there's such a longing in my heart till it hurts

The gentle words you once spoke through the
tenderness of your heart is what keeps me with such
hope your words keep me afloat at a time like this

I can dream on because I believe in your love and I believe in
you. I remember what you said and I'm holding on steadfast

I'd love to hear it spoken again if only I could

But until I see you I may not know just when but I
do know there shall be a time called then.

Deborah Boone

"I Miss You! My Love"

How do I tell you my most adorable husband how much I miss you?

Let me see if it is possible to count all the ways

Can I tell you that I miss you first and foremost because I love you

Is it possible to express all my heart to you as to how precious you
are to me? If so it is one of the many reasons why I miss you so

I miss you because you're near in heart
and thought yet you're far away

I miss you because you are a very dear and vital part of my life.

I miss you because no one can love me as you do

I miss you because I feel secure in your love and your
absence causes my heart to grow fonder of you although
it cries with such a tender yearning for you.

I miss you because without you I'm half and not whole

I miss you because you're the intrigue part of my soul

How can I tell you all the ways I miss you

I miss you because every day we're apart
a precious part of me is missing

I miss you because there's a longing too be hugged that can
only be satisfied by you: in your arms and yours alone

I miss you because you're my inspiration

"I Miss You! My Love"

Can it be possible to tell you all the ways I miss you

Is it possible to share my heart by emptying out all
the reasons of why to love you is to miss you

My heart is full of I miss you's

I miss you because I long to hear the sound of your voice

I miss you because you fill up my senses

I miss you because my life is not happy without you here

I miss you because you're mine and I'm yours

I miss you because you're the love of my life

You are my sunshine on those rainy days

You're my comfort on those lonely days and nights

When I'm weak many times I've felt your strength

I miss you because I can feel your love even in the distant nights

I miss you because you care for me and I
cherish the care I feel from you.

I miss you because there is no other love I'd rather have than yours

I miss you because there is no one that can make me feel
as you do. I come undone at the sound of your name

I miss you because my heart belongs to you;
to my Daniel and my Daniel alone

I miss you for all the reasons you want me
there with you right by your side

I miss you because when I awake in the middle of the
night you are not there to hold me through the night

I miss you because you're my best friend and when I need
a listening ear or a word of advice you're not near

How can I tell you or count all the reasons for why I miss you

Deborah Boone

"I Miss You! My Love" *(continued)*

I miss you most because I love you and aside from all of this I miss you for all the beauty I see, feel, and know that's in you.

I miss you most because I can search this earth and there will never be another perfect match for me just you

I miss you because you're the most important person to me in this whole wide world

I miss you for all the charming ways about you

I treasure your love, My King, my priest, my gift from God above.

"Essence Rare"

I have a treasure given to me by God's divine hand

He is part of the masterpiece that God has so divinely planned

He's the love of my life and that's my God given right

To cherish Him for the rest of my life

He's precious he's sweet He's truly heaven sent

When I think on Him I can't help but to see the
amazing grace of God's great love

You see, He poured into him a portion of Him self.

He blessed and chose Him to be one of God's best

He's a delight to my heart, and as refreshing waters to my soul.

He stands proud and bold as the second captain of my soul

He's faithful, thoughtful, caring and quite a humanitarian

He's precious, He's charming won't stand for anything to harm me.

He's special a rare breed a one of a kind but all mine

I love him you see, He's been there for me

He's faithful and kind and pours out His heart to the master, you
see He says He's mine and He'll cherish me until the end of time

He's my second pair of eyes for He has The
Good Lord's above all seeing eye

"Essence Rare" *(continued)*

He's gentle, He's tender in heart, He's faithful
to me and His heart will never part.

What a treasure to possess this gift of wealth

God has bestowed so favorably upon my breast

He's my priest, my King, my knight in shining armour

He takes interest in me and prays and seeks God
above too so He'll know what's best for me

A man of honor and integrity He's proven His love so measurelessly

I find peace in Him and beauty rare, an extraordinary
gentlemen He's human but rare.

I'm honored to be his queen you see for He is
my King, and that with much sincerity

I truly mean

He's the love of my life the best thing thats ever happened to me

I am His wife (to be) and this surely is a delight to me

To be by His side and spend a short E-tern-it-y

He's the love of my life

The apple of my eye

He's my pride and joy and I don't mind telling the world

My savior sent Him from above

He matched us perfect not just through His love

But through God's very own gift of love

I love you Daniel till the end of time

"The Prince of Tide"

My tide changed when you came into my life

I was fragile, weak, depleted from the sufferings in my life

I could not see the beauty that was once so vibrant in my life

It was covered by the pain that had caused me so much shame

I vowed you see to remain on my own

I pleaded Lord you're able to take good care of me

Just Jesus and me was my prayer and my plead

I could not see the beauty of all He had just for me

A horrible pit He reached down into

He remade me, fashioned me all brand new

He poured in oil and wine anew

Beauty for ashes He arrayed me to look somewhat dazzling

So much beauty He poured into me

No longer do I say Just Jesus and Me

My Prince of Tide has come and from His healing I"ve come undone

I'm amazed at all the handsome charm he wears.

He has helped me to discover a beauty so fair

"The Prince of Tide" *(continued)*

He's my friend, my lover, my husband, my brother (in Christ)

He's devoted and committed to love none other

He took the time to invest in much prayer

His labor not yet completely rewarded

Will tell an untold story because He dared to give up the fight.

God has fashioned me in such beauty you see.

I laugh, I talk, I giggle and can see

All the inward beauty He has caused to be poured into me.

Now I love being just me no longer afraid to say I do thee wed

But boastful and humbly I do pledge

To be thy wife for the rest of my life

Once I could not say the word marriage

It was a language unheard among the usage of my many words

The best that I could do was to say a special friend

But when the Prince of Tide came it broke
the distaste to my heartache

By the spirit of the Lord and the riches of His glory

He has fashioned, molded and shaped me brand new

He sent my true love with healing in His wings

He's my precious King

Now I can't help but sing I love him, I love
him he's my wonderful everything

"You Were There"

You were there when I needed you most

When I felt so all alone didn't know just how to cope

You were there!

You were there when the tears fail and I felt so frail

You were there!

You were there when I was weak and could not stand all alone

I needed to be made strong

You were there!

I heard your voice say you can do it with command
I heard! You say you can be strong and I drew from
the power of strength and I became strong

You were there

You were there when the pains of life took hold
and caused my soul to fold You were there!

You were there when the burdens weighed me down
and the cares of life seemed to overwhelm me

You were there!

I didn't know what to do, you see my troubles were more
than just a few, but you were there to comfort me

"You Were There" *(continued)*

You took charge without saying a word and
on your knees you took on my cares

You were there!

You were there when I felt such pain it
seemed like death was so very near,

But you stepped in and took control of my fears

You took me in your arms and held me close
never a word not once spoken

But in your arms I felt every word for they spoke in
silence to my soul the need I could not have told

I felt the contrary winds that had swept over my soul. But in
your arms, I felt safe. My soul grabbed hold to security and
comfort I found in your love, and it freed me from the struggle
of mind that was so battered. You held me, I felt so protected,
my fears were calmed my body laid arrested in the tenderness
of your arms, and I laid my head upon your chest, I rested.

Such a peace, such a comfort all was made calm once again

I wish it could have last, it went by way to fast, but you were there!

You were there when I felt sick unto death not
a mumbling word did I say to no one.

As my body was wrecked with pain and my
mind filled with anguish once again

Still you were there letting me know how much
you care and assured me you wouldn't leave, but
would be there whenever I need thee

You were there

"You Were There" *(continued)*

Its been months, yet it seems like years

I've waited to see you and just longed to be near you.
Challenges have interfered. Yet you hold me O' so dear

What I've realized the most is in you, I can find
strength to cope whatever maybe happening in my
life your prayers have helped and kept me afloat

You've been there for me

I have found the real meaning of life to truly exist

O not just by the spirit of God alone

But a real world I can call my own, I'm at home in you

You are my world and my world is complete
in you because I exist in you.

To the love of my life with blessings from the

Father above

Deborah Boone

"My Eternal Love"

You're special to me and I know that this you must see

I've wondered at times what you must think of me

You see me when I'm down but you know I'll come around

You hear my laughter and it just doesn't
matter what others opinions may be

I write stories about you and me what an
extraordinary individual you are to me

You know my thoughts yet nothing has ever made you depart

No matter how hard I've fought to struggle through

I'm amazed at all the beauty I find in you.

I smile, chuckle, laugh at the mention of your name

I'm swept off my feet my heart just honestly can't contain
the joy, the ecstasy at the mere mention of your name

I love you more today because you stayed with me in all my pain.

Even when it was a strain to just hold on and maintain the day

Sometimes the battle was so intense Only Jesus knew. To me at
times it made no sense how one could suffer and just not give in

But never a mind did I have to quit

You were there and you shared my pain

"My Eternal Love" *(continued)*

I'm sure at times you felt the strain

But never not once did you say Deborah I've changed

You spoke a word, O yes I heard and I held on with everything in me.

But there were times when I wondered what did He think about me

I learned this one thing is true I am stronger
because of you. I love you.

"My Extroadinary You!"

I have a love that is like none other

Its unique you see

Its both you and me

On my worst days he can cause my face to break forth
into a blush that spreads into an amazing smile

My eyes begin to sparkle and a glow suddenly appears

The magic of all his charm brightens my day with cheer

When I think on my most extroadinary you

I feel fulfilled in heart and mind

Even when feeling blue

You amaze me with all your

beauty rare

It's hard to define all I feel

deep down inside

Words are hard, challenging

to say the least, to really define

Just what you mean to me

I'm proud to know you are no match no where can one be

found To me, you are truly unique and you
bring out the very best in me.

"Since You Went Away"

Since you went away my world seems to say

I'm blue without you

A part of me is missing and I need you

I need you to strengthen, revive, and refresh me anew

No one knows me better than you

I need to hear your voice to bring comfort to me

Through the tender sound of your voice my heart will rejoice again

Its lonely without you, come on home, our house was intended for 2

With Jesus in our view we can start our lives anew

Take me by my hand, lead me into the
presence of our King, let's live again

Let's pray and tell him about everything

He's the master of our souls

He knows how to restore the charm of love in our souls

He can make our hearts sing a new song

It will wash away where ever we went wrong

Come on home! I need you to help me raise our children

"Since You Went Away" *(continued)*

To paint a picture on the canvass of their hearts of
just how God intended for families not to depart

Reach deep inside of me as only you can

You'll see its possible for our love to be strengthened again

Since you went away

I've fallen down. I need help to get up again

I know its possible. We can win again with Jesus at the helm

I'm praying for you! Lord open His eyes. Correct his sight.
Teach him what is right by showing Him your light

I need you to come home again.

Lets set things aright

we can soar together to a

brand new height

Lets make it right!

Why not tonight?

To those who are apart may this writing
encourage hope in your hearts

"A Romantic Interlude"

What about tonight? Can I plan a date with my wife?

Why not tonight?

When the heaven is open with such moonlight

What about tonight?

The breeze is singing such a soft melody

The trees are swaying saying take advantage of this moment in time

Ah! I hear the string of my heart singing

A love song with such a sweet melody

Why not tonight?

Lets pour out our hearts in love the mood is just right

We hardly ever talk of the things we love most

We boast of our troubles and of how we need to get over

But why not tonight?

Lets make it right

A quiet moment shared for 2

an interesting conversation from your point of view

Tell me what's in your heart and I'll share what's in mine.

Only let it be this magical moment in mind

"A Romantic Interlude" *(continued)*

Feel my senses with your love

Cause my love to be renewed for 2

Let me be strengthened by the power of your love

Through the words spoken to my soul

Allow me to grow old with you by my side

Lets turn the years back and reminisce on
the wonderful memories in time

Why not tonight?

The mood is just right?

Candlelight for 2

I won't mind sitting across the table from you

You'll be my lovely view

I just need you to talk to me

renew our love again

Gain a new future and then we will fall in love all over again

Why not tonight?

P.S.
To couples who don't take or have the time to just share. I pray this
will help you to open up and build a brand new day.

"My Wedding Nite"

I am a bride all dressed in white

Purity has been my God given right

To abstain from sin to please Him in the end

I am a bride all dressed in white

I give myself to thee on this our wedding nite

I vowed to love, to cherish, and honor for life

This Holy Man of God who walks this Christian life

He is my groom and well pleased am I indeed

For He'll love me and treasure me because I aim to please

Adorned in the glory of Gods Holy Matrimony

An example, He has made me and privileged me to have
one of His very best out of God's treasure chest

My room is adorned with the beauty of God

For He chose this love and foretold our wedding plans

Yes! This is His delight His daughter in white

He can show off His light that doth shine so bright.

That if you will but wait for the Masters plan

"My Wedding Nite" (continued)

You will share a lifetime by His divine plan

Yes! I am a bride dressed in white

My Father's in Heaven great delight.

To God Be the Glory

To all the single women who desire to marry Mr. Right and expect a happy life.

"Till Then"

We've known each other for so long

It seems like a lifetime our hearts are filled with such fond memories

We've been patiently waiting till then ---

We fought a fight that has ushered us in

To a deeper level of love that just won't bend

We've shared hard times together,

We weathered many a storms

Sometimes our boat seemed to drift with alarm

But anchored in the depth of our souls

Was a passion that held us to our hope

That one day in time we would see the Son shine and
fulfill our will that place in time called til then

"A Hidden Secret Chamber"

I have a love, but I cannot tell it

It's just not time to share it.

But way down deep inside of me I can travel to
a secret chamber that resides in me

In this quiet place of solitude and thoughts

I can open up my heart and release my best thoughts

Like precious oils that flow from the vines

Like exotic perfumes that fills any room

I have a love all my own

He is precious and possess all my heart

In the walls of my mind

I can't count the many times

I've thought on his name

and still I feel the same

Excited, to know what I have gained

I have a secret chamber that's a far away place

I can enter into it whether day or night

I can dream of a time and place that seems so divine

"A Hidden Secret Chamber" *(continued)*

Moments shared by 2 filled with love and laughter to

I can recall at times days gone by

When at first we met

The beauty, the sweetness that sweep my heart

When first I heard your name

Such delight came from within its left me smiling from then til now

How awesome I thought

How powerful in deed

You mean God gave me someone

that made one feel so proud

I still can't help but to smile

"Things Are Better"

Its still very hard to be apart from you

Yet in my heart I know you're near

Still the distance at time seems unbearable

To love you so is hard when we are so close and yet so far apart

To say I miss you doesn't do justice

To say I long for you in a way it is a blessing

To know my heart cherishes you so

Still there's a pain, an aching in my heart

We're apart and my heart cries out for you

To reach in the distant and be able to feel you

I know you're closer than I think but I don't know how
to tell my heart and mind to cause it to believe it would
bring a great relief to me and in return to you

How so, I could reach through the distance and touch you

I could tell you words that would pour out of my heart and soul

Words that would bring a smile to your face a comfort to your heart

Words that would strengthen, refresh and revive you

The sound of the sweetness would melt your heart
with a kindness that would kindle a warm fire of
a renewal of a first time acquaintance

"Things Are Better" *(continued)*

It would wrap you like a blanket on a cold
nite that would bring a coziness

It would make lonely nites sweet and peaceful

It would cause a rest that only can be described
by our hearts and our hearts alone

Things are getting better because time is
drawing nearer to be together

Deborah Boone

"An Appointed Time"

God had a plan for you to be joined with me in this lifetime

He diligently sought to full-fill your heart

Yet to design his perfect will for your life and mine

He suffered trials and some tests to endure (Daniel)

Now I can see why it had to be

Because He truly was grooming me

To pay the price to be your wife

To know the worth of a vessel God's heart delight

I went through the fire, the floods too

Sometimes I could hardly swim but He kept my focus still on you.

No devil He declared would stop His master plan

And so with great care of a rescue He came

He showed me a sign a rainbow in my sky

He said it is set for thee appointed time

Anchored deep in body I am

Planted by the Masters divine plan

He chose me and arrayed me as gold tried in the fire

He knew I'd have to help with the souls appointed for you to win

"An Appointed Time" *(continued)*

Sometimes my burdens seemed hard but He
assured me the cost would be worth it all

He said I've chosen you to be His bride not only to be by His side

But to fulfill m prophesy I've desired

A perfect pair I've made you to be

Now take this my prophesy

Go forth in me cause the enemy to flee

Bring home for me souls for my Kingdom

With Jesus you can win

and at the end you will see

Heaven's gates open up to thee

For such a great price you've paid to gain the
lost because Jesus paid such great cost

Deborah Boone

Part III
"A Mother's Heart"

"A Mother's Love"

So precious and dear to me this love, a
gift, God imparted to my heart

I bore you, I carried you, watched over you,
taught you, watched you bloom

From infancy when you laid on my breast

when I held you close

In every new quest

the love of a mother constantly put to test

Somehow the years so rapidly rushed by

Before I knew it you took hold deep down inside

I sought you, I sighed, I cried, Jesus was my guide

He was ever faithful as He stood by my side

The greater the challenge the closer to my bosom I held you

I feared a night would come so dark you
would not be able to find your way

I tossed, I turned, some nights no sleep

Some days the heart so heavy I could not eat

Often, weeping was my meat

I searched high and reached low

"A Mother's Love" *(continued)*

Too many valleys encompassed my soul

So many a times out of my control

Tattered and torn was my poor soul

The love you searched for was always near

Begging and pleading, I cried, look here(!) my dear

Blinded by sins enchanted moments and fantasies,

void of understanding, caught up in a world, you could never fit

Lost in time, precious memories fading out of our minds

Behold! Look! Now see what was missed, missed, missed,

A Mothers tender love, dissed, dissed, dissed

Deborah Boone

"God's Gift To The World"

A Mother

What is a Mother?

M	-	Monumental
o	-	One (who's)
t	-	tender –
h	-	hearted
e	-	ever
r	-	relentless (in love)

A Mother is a gift from God. She has the attributes of
God Himself wrapped tied and poured into her

Making and creating her to be one extroadinary individual

There is nothing that can compare to the profound
and astonishing nature, character, gifts and innate
abilities wrapped in this glorified flesh – woman

We all know that God is love and that He is longsuffering,
patient, kind, tenderhearted ever providing ways to
meet our needs and He's a caretaker for us.

When we hurt we can run to Him and He will mother us because
He has a mothering nature as well as the nature of a father

"God's Gift To The World" *(continued)*

He holds us when we're broken. When we cry and
don't know what to do he consoles us.

Now isn't that just like a mother? Ever tender and so gentle in nature

When we're unable to go beyond our dark nights and lonely days
it is a mother's gentle voice of wisdom that propels you on.

Somehow she speaks strength, and out of her
wisdom comes the strength and assurance that
I can make it. But isn't that just like God?

We don't see it, but through the advice and instructions
she poured or pours into us it guides us through
our darkest nights and loneliest day.

But isn't that just like God

We can turn to Mothers to share our most intimate feelings
and concerns and we know she has our best interest at heart

Even if its not what we want to hear. Yet a real mother
will tell you the read deal. But isn't that just like God.

She's ever faithful. Always willing to go beyond the call of
duty. Always sacrificing her time, her personal life, her body
in strength, whether sick or well. She's deprived of a right to
be selfish once in a while to take time to be good to herself for
she is that human sacrifice committed and devoted to perfect
your life and strengthen you in your weakest moments.

She's deprived of having a life that she has well earned and deserves.
Instead she seeks to strengthen her relationship with her children.
They're the apple of her eyes. But again isn't that just like God.

Doesn't He sacrifice His feelings too. Do you realize how
He goes beyond the call of duty to embrace us.

Can you see the side of God that's a mother
through the attributes of a Mother?

Her very nature is the incarnate nature of God. A Mother is one
who is tenderhearted ever relentless in love. She takes any kind
of abuse but she'll protect and fight for her babies. So it is with
God. God takes time to hear our faintest cry, to heal our broken

Deborah Boone

"God's Gift To The World" *(continued)*

hearts and hurts, mend our wounded spirits, embrace us through His love and whether we desire it or not refuses to let us go. He wrapped His very nature in this human flesh and created a manual in the heart of woman that intensifies the instructions of mothering through God's given creative power called innate ability. He poured a love in our heart to parent even as He became a parent He wasn't always a parent and neither were we. But one day He had a son called Jesus born of a virgin woman called Mary ordained by God.

He taught us the value of family. Now there is another side to a mother. She knows how to scold when you're wrong. She knows how to push you out on a limb to teach you to fly that is to say force the creative potential in you out that you dare to chance.

But that's the fathering side of a mother. It's the authoritative side of God, the Father wrapped up in her fleshly nature

She knows how to discipline and how much time is necessary to perfect what you're being disciplined for so you'll become perfected. But isn't that just like God. In the end mother has poured all herself into you and you're all grown up:

Hopefully refined and a crown of glory and honor to the parents

How awesome is it that God entrusted in our hands a precious lump of clay to mold and make and fashion

What a wondrous thing to have sculptured one's life

We've been blessed to have the greatest gift
life can offer placed in our hands.

As God created Adam and Eve so has He in like manner allowed us to create thee. We've sculptured created, formed, shaped the very essence of who you are to be. A vital part of your, life loving, woven, from the heart of a mother

and to the heart of many

Now isn't she just like God.

The only true and wise God.

To God Be all the Glory

Part IV
"The Winner In You"!

"My Life Is All The Better"

My life is all the better because of Jesus and you

God gave me hope through believing in you

In you I found the strength to love again

In you I found the courage to trust once again

Yes! My life is all the better because of Jesus and you

When God gave me you I found truth in future hope I could not see

I discovered in you the beauty of life to live again and be me

In you I found pure love, unselfish, unbias, and totally new

I realized the future was not as bleak as it had appeared

For there was shone a light deep within
that was so bright so illuminating

It was the love in your heart for me that
made my path once again clear

Your love was shining so bright it took all the fright right out of me

Dare I trust a man again

Could I see myself willing to take on that risk again

I can live alone, all on my own for by myself I
am safe and there is no fear on my own

With man I don't know if I can be strong

"My Life Is All The Better" *(continued)*

But I discovered a beauty I had never known

Through you and Jesus I've began to bloom again

A rose so sweet of a fragrance and the gracefulness beauty rare

Yes! I'm blessed. My life is all the better because of you and Jesus

You committed your love to me though yet
I wasn't visible for you to see

Still you told me you loved me and quote "My eyes are only for you"

I was the only one you chose to see

You said I love you and I want to marry you

Still yet tender but sure of wanting your love and to love you

I whole heartedly surrendered

You had made a decision for you have great wisdom

You knew what you desired and I was the prize

Chosen by God and endorsed by you

A journey began that was long overdue

I'm beautiful within and I know no more ugly

My rose petals has opened up and fully developed

Wow! All I can say is what a change within

My life is all the better because of you and Jesus

The beauty in you has ignited in me

and little do you know I took heed to every word

astonished amazed but by His grace

I'm totally opened in a brand new way

I can say proudly I love you! I do! It is my testimony

I discovered me too (in you)

Deborah Boone

"My Life Is All The Better" *(continued)*

Its the truth and every word is pure

That's how great an affect your love has impacted my life

Now when I go to the mirror I see for 2

I see me and I see you. I see the change that has taken place in me.

The mirror captures the beauty of your love so dear

I see you though I see you not I see you in me the part
of your heart that tenderly transformed me

I see the beauty of all you are and I see the
wonder of God's given true love.

Dare I tell you how I long to be with thee

Shall I tell you of the countless hours spent reminiscing on thee?

I love you today more than yesterday

And for the rest of my life I do vow to be your wife

I love you, to have you, to cherish you in
this life for the rest of my life

I treasure you God's gift of beauty rare

My life is all the better because I have you

And in you I found this rich treasure of love forever

All that I do is about you

My life has blossomed and bloomed because of dear, you

So, Honey, just know I'm here for you. I'll always be by your
side to love you with my gentle arms opened wide.

You are special to me

You're the intrigue part of my soul

When I see you I see me and there is no better view of life than
for you to take me as thy bride your lawful wedded wife

Through you I see such a devoted love

"My Life Is All The Better" (continued)

Daniel, I promise to cherish you as God's gift from above

Words can never express the love in my heart for you.

But thanks be unto God that you chose me to love the best

I love you honey, There could never be another. It's you
I want and I desire to have and long for and need

My heart is committed to you

"To A Very Special Friend"

In appreciation for the many qualities that
make you a wonderful friend

For sharing the ups and downs of life

You are the sunshine of my days

and the rainbow of my sad days

For always being there to listen

Trying hard to understand and somehow knowing just how to help

You are the rose among the thorns of my life

For giving your time and your interest unselfishly

You shelter me from the storms of life

My friend you are the best part of hard times

The brightest of good times

My friend I offer you this expression of my love and appreciation

You are God's gift to me.

"I Made It"

My Father, a few days ago I climbed up to the
highest mountain I've ever known

I dwelt in your warm and tender embrace

I imagined the joy and excitement leaping
in your heart for I feel it too

I could picture the sparkle in your eyes for
they were set with such a glow

The excitement in your voice was strong, loud, and clear with
the anticipation of something good was on the horizon

How wonderful and glorious to know your
heart was so full of rejoicing

I can imagine angels cheering saying come on,
come on, you've made it. You've made it.

You finally won the race

Hence forth is laid up for you riches untold

Yes! A celebration had taken place then for now

For you foresaw today

You knew it afar off when we first meet

God how awesome is this place

How breathtakingly awesome

"I Made It" *(continued)*

It is as though I sit and the t.v. is showing
some wondrous tourist place

Some island of enchantment that I see before my very eyes

Only this is real, this is true the beauty of your heart
in thoughts unfolding in reality unto me

I see your hand, your signature, inscribed in the clouds

And everywhere I look is so much beauty as I behold the
signature of God inscribed on all things in my new world

I'm at home at last

I'm free from my past

I feel my Father's warm embrace

Caressing me and welcoming me from a long awaited journey

I can hear my Father's voice filled with ecstasy

O' How He has long awaited this moment
such patience has He endured

All the smiles of glad tidings and good cheer are
here surrounding me in my new world

Jesus is here taking me in the comfort of His arms

My Dad standing so tall and proud

The Holy Spirit is proclaiming lets celebrate for finally

I've arrived

This my New World is a secret place where only
the trinity and myself are allowed in.

It's a place promised to me of long ago.

A place where peace and happiness makes there abode

It's quiet here, so peaceful, all is at rest.

No thoughts of tomorrow or yesterday gone by.

"I Made It" (continued)

It's a world that fills every fiber of your being
and awakens your senses to true reality

It's the joys of Jesus and the benefits of suffering

A place at last I've searched high and low to be

The presence here causes my soul to dwell at ease.

My mind is clear, my spirit is refreshed, my soul
overflows with His goodness and mercies

All memories of the past has vanished and taken
wings like a bird and fled far far away

The joy and peace here is indescribable, how
magnificent are the stars at night

Such beauty that surpasses my mind

The midnight blue sky sleeping and at rest, filled
with so many stars glowing everywhere.

The Kaos of the day has fled and every enemy and
foe has tucked its tail and away they're gone

The breeze is so gentle so warm it clothes you
like a blanket, all safe, cozy and warm.

The stillness of the night it speaks to my soul

Saying no longer my child will you have to search high and low

For I have come and taken out time to fill the longing of your soul

You are now sitting so high up on this mountain looking over the
sleepy blue ocean and the waterfalls down cascading the mountains

The deer are roaming, drinking fresh water to quince
their thirst from a long hot blistering day

Ahh! The beauty I see. The moon is full so round
and bright given off its heavenly light

The trees rustling in the wind enjoying the refreshing breeze

"I Made It" *(continued)*

I see trees so strong, so tall, standing firmly
planted very deep in the soil

No wonder God likens us unto trees of
righteousness planted by the Lord

All is at rest. I find comfort and strength. I feel reborn again

Ahh this secret place hidden so far away

But I've climbed to the top and discovered all
the beauty hidden through my troubles.

Dad I've made it. I've made it (dad is my God) I dwell
in the secret place of the most High God

I'm covered under the shadow of His wings, The Almighty God.

Here there is no hustle no bustle, its only the
here and now away from troubles

To God be the Glory

"I Am A Somebody"

I was a nobody until God found me and made me a somebody

He took His creative ingenious power and His healing oil,
and once again in my life went to work resculpturing me

I was humpty dumpty who sat on the wall and I had a great fall

I was broken tattered, wounded, and torn so often I was scorned

But by the grace of God Jesus laid His eyes on me
and saw what no other man could see

He saw beauty beneath the ashes that I felt was my ruin

He smiled, He said my child your life is not beyond repair

He said there's a beauty side to life that you know not
of and on the other side of your so many struggles

You'll live and not die and you'll preach and
teach the gospel as you cry aloud

I didn't see it, how it could be so my life was
so full of troubles don't you know

He told me the Son will shine again. I'll live because He lives
and I will proclaim an untold story of the victory I've gained

He said you'll snatch souls out of hell for me

You will heal the sick and raise the dead

"I Am A Somebody" (continued)

Because up from the grave (spiritual and
emotional grave) you have been raised

I could see no future

Every day was a struggle to just hold on to God's unchanging hand

He alone was my watchman He cared for my soul

He told me I was in heart pure as gold

I couldn't see it, neither could I receive it
because my troubles had laid me so low

I heard my master saying unto me

You have the victory and victories to come

I sighed, I cried I wondered what had I done

Show me the way where I've done wrong

He said unto me you're precious don't you see, you're a rare
gem that I've chosen to bare hardship for other souls

You're mine saith Jesus to me and you're the apple of my eye

Nothing I can't do, Nothing I won't do for thee

You're favored in my sight and you are my delight

He snatched me out of the grave where I laid so low

He filled my cup with joy that of the Holy Ghost

My feet began to dance again

My hands went to clapping my arms went to flapping as
I moved my feet to the beat of this great victory

He pulled me through the fire that blazed with such vehement heat

He changed me from the old to a brand new me

He put pep in my steps, a smile on my face

Now I'm abounding by God's great grace

"I Am A Somebody" *(continued)*

He dried my tears and chased my broken heart away

Now I'm standing at what I once couldn't face

He dressed me in white for this was His great delight

He smiled and said I'm pleased with thee

Now I have began to see the brand new me He's made over again

His glory proclaims such a great untold story in my life

How I made it on over I've won this great fight

Jesus has and He yet is putting the devil to flight

He's enabled me to stand and be more like His light

I shine bright where I was once dim. I have
a hunger and a thirst deep within.

To tell the lost souls just come on in. You can
win, you can win with Jesus in the end.

My best is yet to come. For I have stood my test. He promised
me great victory and I'm standing in faith to see the great
cloud of His glory showering blessings upon me.

Deborah Boone

"Adversity"

Adversity has many facets

Adversity wears many faces

But one thing about adversity

It serves a powerful purpose

Adversity can be seen as good

Adversity can be seen as bad

But one thing about adversity it is a power it is a powerful force

Adversity can make you, shape you, mold you

That is if you'll let it

Adversity can cause you to grow under pressure

If you will let it

Adversity will cause you to bow your knees and
pray because adversity is a powerful force

Adversity can humble you

If you'll let it

Adversity can work in your favor if you'll let it

Adversity has a purpose it serves

It can make you or break you.

"Adversity" *(continued)*

Adversity can redefine you by those wonderful
days I call character building days

Adversity then can strengthen you all alone from deep within

Adversity is seen as an enemy that turns in our
favor to challenge us in the end to win.

"The Best Of Me"

I have a friend who sticks with me through thick and thin

He's ever faithful

He's that kind of a friend when I'm down He comes around

A word to the wise He imparts deep down inside

When I'm blue for some reason He knows just
what to say to chase my gray sky away

True to the end He'll ever be

Yes! I have a friend

He's precious indeed

I know I can always depend on Him

He's there for me through the thick and thin

He assures me Deborah you can win

I love my friend, He's so special to me

He takes time to genuinely pray to provide the care I need

He's the sweetest person I've ever known

Its hard to define just how kind

So I call him my Extroadinary You:

"The Best Of Me" *(continued)*

He's always thinking of a way to make life better for 2

I love his view of life it reflects his charm with such delight

You see He brings out the very best of me.

I love him for all the days and nights

Such great sacrifice He's paid

I try to study ways in which I can repay

For a friend so dear is a treasure of a lifetime and I hold him dear

Yes! He brings out the best in me.

"Anticipation"

The winner in me is anticipating something good is about to happen

Anticipation is the comfort needed when all around says it can't be

Anticipation is the fire that ignites my soul with joy

It helps to breakthrough every barrier and every foe

Anticipation says I sense within something good is about to happen

We may not know all together how or when

But we know in the end we will win.

Yes! Anticipation can be a wonderful friend

It can help to calm a raging sea

It can tell your senses just hang on in

Yes, anticipation is what we need

When the adrenalin is running low and you feel like
throwing in the towel because nothing shows up

But anticipation says be patient, Hey lets wait,
something I feel is about to turn for my good

I can feel a fleet of joy deep down within

Its telling me be strong just hang on in

Lets see what's at the end

Ahh my friend you're going to win

"Somewhere In The Night"

Somewhere in the night when everything is quiet and oh so very still

I feel the silence of your love calling still

I hear the beating of the heart whispering sweet thoughts

I feel the joy of knowing you're mine and mine alone

A smile breaks out and a tender tear sometimes appear

I'm touched to know that you love and hold me Oh so dear

I'm moved at the long-sufferance and care so precious so pure

My heart cries out in gratitude and such respect and appreciation

It longs to tell you of every heartache since you've been away

The joy I feel of knowing you're near

O how I want to tell you that you're so dear

My eyes long to look into your eyes and tell
you of all the beauty I see inside

My heart cries out for you to know just
how much you truly mean to me

I feel so honored to be yours

For years I have so many thoughts just stored

But what I long to tell you the most is how precious you are

"Somewhere In The Night" *(continued)*

You see you're the one I adore

I just long to be near you to awake each
morning and know you're there

To say goodnight and enjoy the peacefulness
and the beauty of the night

Just to awake and watch you even asleep

O how pleased I would be

I'm ready to pour out all my love upon thee

To lavish you and spoil you is my earnest desire deep inside of me

I want to show you the royalty you deserve to
have by allowing me to just be me

I want all that I feel to flow out from inside of me

Things stored up kept through time by fond memories

I want to share my life with you

Be that someone special you can confide in

I want to live the rest of my life walking side by side just
you being a part of me and as we age and time goes by
I want us to remember the best years of our lives

I want you to know I'm truly honored to be your bride

Daniel maybe you know and maybe you don't but
I take great pride in being chosen by you

I also take great pride to do and to submit
when I hear what you request

I love you none the less

I'm anxious to know you from inside out

I love your boldness

I love your stand to be right

"Somewhere In The Night" *(continued)*

You don't even know it but I smiled with delight

You didn't see it and could not have known

But the truth be told

I honestly love you and so I want you to be your self
and I'm sure you will but one thing I do know

I love you greater still

I've grown and gained such a great respect for you if only
you knew. I believe you'd blush through and through

I'll never flatter you but, I'll say what's on my mind. I
believe we have a friendship, its one of a kind

I've never known a love so pure and so divine

I just wanted to take this pen to express from deep within
that as time has gone by my love has grown deeply inside

I want you to know I don't believe there's nothing you
could say that would cause me to draw away

I realize this one thing the only thing that matters is
love. For me to love you and for you to love me.

"I Gave Him My Best"

Life has a way on the journey we take

It causes twist and turns we are not often willing to take

But there's one journey that requires such a risk

It takes us into the depths where our saviour sits

Storms arise, winds blow sometimes the
rain beats vehemently at our door

Can we stand sometimes we say?

Because we feel shaken and out of place

But there's a saviour who sits on high

He vowed ever to be at our side

What ever the test life my bring

Our saviour will cause us to follow a stream

That lead us safely beneath His wings

Here we find peace and rest we need

Strengthened and refreshed as we kneel at His feet

The comfort we need, may often take wings

We'll find ourselves in His will

Able to stand another storm as we learn to be still

"I Gave Him My Best" *(continued)*

He teaches us wondrous things of His love

We learn to abide and dwell with our hearts
and minds stayed on Him in love

Yes! Life has a way of offering us twist and turns and winding roads

But these are the test He has chosen to make us our best

He pours in oil and wine anew

As he restores and refreshes us brand new

And in the end we can win

For the Saviour doth keep us safe in Him

Deborah Boone

"My Joy, My Delight"

I have a heavenly Father whom I call all my own

He sits up high and looks down low

He watches carefully over my soul

He sees and know me inside out

So when that Ole devil the thief tries to take me out

He teaches my soul to bless the Lord for the wonders He has unfold.

In the midst of adversity He causes me to be still

He teaches me of His love and grace and mercies so real

I find in him a place where I can kneel

And tell my saviour just how I feel

He welcomes me with open arms

He sits attentive to my needs as I give Him alms

Full of compassion and love is He

He pours it out without measure to meet my needs

I and my Father in Heaven agree

He planted a seed inside of me

So often I come on bending knees

Not just with my hands out in need

"My Joy, My Delight" *(continued)*

But to pour out my love on Him this He needs and He doth receive

You see He has a heart that feels just as ours

He has needs to meet by this His treasure

Earthen vessels He has blessed us to be

I declare I'm made to inhabit His praise

So I bow on my knees O most High

In Holy reverence and honor to receive by thy bride

With great honor and pride I pour out from deep inside

Gratitude and praise O most High

For worthy is the Lamb who sits on high

Who vowed one day He would come take away His bride

To cherish Her and love her and sit her on high

For He paid the cost for us the church He brought this

Purchased by His blood for us at no cost.

"The Future"

I see a future in sight

Oh how lovely and what a peaceful sight

Its light doth shine Oh so brightly

Its covered by the rainbow God's promise from heaven above

Yes! I see a future

A happy, happy, me

For I have a promise Jesus has given to me

Its filled with hope, prosperity and peace

Its sealed with His pen for He has written within the scrolls of time

There ain't no devil that can win

Yes! I see a future its filled with love, joy and a brighter tomorrow

Its sweet to think on how precious it is

There is a tomorrow

a rainbow of God's best

Its filled with God's sweet sweet rest

A place He has chosen to reward me as a faithful servant

A place He has chosen to reward

"The Future" *(continued)*

To the East to the West to the North He spake
give up and to the South hold not back

To the heart of the earth He commanded it to come up

All the hidden treasures saying come forth, come forth

Throughout the land He has called forth to cease and
enjoy God's great gift of opportunity to be.

Deborah Boone

"Things Will Get Better"

Sometimes there are dark clouds that seem to
have a way of creeping into our lives

Often it happens suddenly without warning

But behind every dark cloud there is the dawning of another day

Somehow, someway, things change

And things do get better

As incredible as it may seem

the darkest night is the dawning

of a new day bright

Life is full of uncertainties but we learn to master
the things we feel that just ought not be

In those times of painful experiences

We learn the lessons that life has to offer

And if we can but wait/

things will get better

Darkness says no way out that is what it loves best to dictate

But if we can have faith or just be positively optimistic
we will see our courage begin to rise

The voice of Faith will speak and say I don't know but some how

"Things Will Get Better" *(continued)*

Things will get better if we will wait a little while

Life is full of ups and downs We don't always know
how to swim so that we won't drown

But one thing for sure is you can dare to be a winner
and if you dare to believe that it can be

Things will get better

We don't always understand and sometimes we
wrestle with change but once we learn to accept the
challenge it brings then we can receive the change

That things will get better

We may not know how, we may not know
when but somewhere before it ends

Things have a way of turning around and things do get better

So we will take the bitter cup that life has to offer
for after we drink we are amazed as we think

Things truly did get better

So just know there is an end and in it you win

Because things do get better.

Deborah Boone

"To A Very Special Friend"

In appreciation for the many qualities that
make you a wonderful friend

For sharing the ups and downs of life

You are the sunshine of my days and the rainbow of my sad days

For always being there to listen

Trying hard to understand and somehow knowing how to help

You are the rose among the thorns of my life

For giving your time and your interest unselfishly

You shelter me from the storms of life

My special friend you are the best part of hard times

The brightest of good times

My friend I offer you this expression of my love and appreciation

"You are God's gift to Me"

Part V
Creating My World

"A Blistery Winter's Day"

As I looked outside of my window

What a joyful sight it was to see

It was my favorite time of the year

It was cold outdoors because it was December
24th the day before Christmas

The wind was howling, the trees though now
bare swayed in the cold blistery wind

Snow had began to fall enough so that the ground
once dull from its beautiful summery green was
snow covered in a beautiful blanket of white

The trees was glistening from Mr. Jack Frost

Some places the snow had been removed and tossed

Ahh the air was fresh

The cold had ushered in a purifying scent in the air
that was most welcoming to the nostrils.

It was a perfect scene that mother nature in all her
splendor had provided for all who'd dare to go out

She spoke to the cold and said Winter's here
at last time has come to pass

To those far and near she hurled her cry

Button up or you'll be cold wrap warm the days of sun is shoned

"A Blistery Winter's Day" (continued)

Its my season to show off my glory

Its time for me to shine forth

I'm white and bright

I'm beautiful like the stars at night

Its often much of me to spread and share pretty much everywhere

I have a magnificent beauty all my own

Every flake a different shape

Soft as I can be

Delicious tasting to others yet a frown to another

I can cause you to sit by the fire and snuggle up

Get all cozy and warm

I can cause you to see the beauty of my winter wonderland

I can bring you inviting moments of a good
book and a hot cup of chocolate coco.

I can even cause you to sit close to the one you love the most

Or offer you cover with your significant other

Sometimes I provide magical moments like cold feet reaching
my loves warm feet - saying lets share - your feet are warm
let me put mine next to yours and help me be warm

Yes! I'm a very different season. My season offers
those special magical moments that bring comfort,
indoor charm and beauty and warm cozy nights

Sometimes I provide lovely snow-flocked trees

Beautiful icicles hanging on trees and houses just to see and
suddenly everywhere all around town is all snow-white and bright

Enjoy me while you can for I offer everyone my adventure land

"A Blistery Winter's Day" *(continued)*

There's sleigh rides and time to ski on slopes
tobogganing and even there are those who dare to
swim in their skin they're bathing suits oh so thin

Some play in snow building snowmen, others snowballs, yet I
provide others the creative art of sculpturing ice figurines

I create snow cap mountains and Antarctic cold

To the animals some hibernate others
boisterously and bold fight the cold

So you know I give the privilege to a few
a wonderful romantic stroll

Yes! I am all together lovely

I'm cold, I'm snow, I'm Jack Frost and so much more

You can see me from your indoors or some
stroll with me in this great out of doors

You can go mountain climbing

Ice fishing and animal hunting too

And if all of these are not enough

You can invite family and friends over for
a toasty marshmallow roast

Yes! I'm a special fun time of the year

I am a season all my own

To the bold, daring and brave I offer a wonderful carriage
ride in the snow best known as Central Park in New York.

Enjoy me! Have fun on these cold blistery winter wonderful days.

"The Dawning of The Day"

There's a quiet still voice that walks to you
through the wee hours of the night

It wants to tell you all that's right

Throughout the night, He's the watchman of my soul

He whispers gently to my soul Get up, Get up! Awake O' my soul

It is I, it is I, come sit in my throne room I
bid thee come in the door is open

You're welcome to just walk in

As He sits on the throne and ask for sweet aromas of praise and
acculades of thanksgiving is rendered from gratitude of heart

He smiles and embraces the inadequate praises I do raise

His heart is moved for He knows the sound of every one
of His children and just where they can be found

Excitement runs through my veins for in His
presence I'm special and He reigns

He teaches me of His ways and guides me
through the dawning of the day

In His presence nothing else matters. Just the two of our hearts

A welcome surprise it always seems to be for the dawning
of day begins a new beginning again you see

Its filled with all the spices of life, wrapped up in the
gift of praise from the entrance of the throne room

"The Dawning of The Day" (continued)

Yes, its a secret place where no time is known,
no watch is there to say hurry on

My face does so eagerly embrace these special
moments alone with my savior

For it is something about His quietness that brings
such a stirring to my rather be bed rested soul

There's a sweetness, a beauty, that's so indescribable,
only the throne room can express it

We're as close as close can be

He says come in, lend me your ear

He whispers sweet things to my soul as He
unfolds His heart more precious than gold

Suddenly the time has passed by without noticing
how or when the night fled away and gave pass for
the dawning of a new bright and glorious day

It was time well spent with Jesus and me all alone
in the whole big wide world don't you see.

I was cradled in His arms, I was illuminated by all His charms
as He attentively listened. I yielded, safe from all harm

The angels were there, O' no not in view but
they stood all around in heavens view.

They covered me from head to toe so that
O'l serpent could do no hurt

They waited till the end and escorted me back safely free from sin

You see I was washed whiter than snow,
given a brand new white robe

The old garment I wore could stand no more

Jesus came and He entered the room He
restored my soul and gave me more
A new life never known before.

"The Dawning of The Day" *(continued)*

It was the Master I had sought didn't know He was already there.
As I tried to compare the old and the new
it had started to tare, the walls the bricks fell 2 by 2

Jesus was rendering me all brand new

The old had died and tried to surface back up but with
just one cup of oil and wine a new destiny stood now
in view. Now if I drink this cup I can move beyond
the old view and enter into what is brand new

All is well for my saviour is near

He leads, He guides, He calms all fears

There is no need to worry or be dismayed the saviour is awaiting
this brand new glorious day. The angels of the Lord shall usher
me in and all I've ever awaited will be found safe within

To God be the Glory

Deborah Boone

"The Glory of God's Gift To Write"

Its fascinating to me to see all the beauty
He has created deep within me

For when I write I can escape in life all the
hustles, bustles and the cares of life

I can create my own world with a stroke of a pen
and let life flow out from deep down within

I'm filled with beauty rare sometimes it tries
to blind me with this ole life's cares

But I can paint a picture if I dare

I travel places far away through envisioning my great imagination

I visit places I've never been

I can see faces I've never known

I can dare to dream a world all of my own

I can choose to share or remain all alone

But whatever the choice its all mine and mine alone.

"How Splendid Is The Night"

Have you ever gazed up at the heavenly view of the sky at night?

Did your senses pick-up an awareness of the city asleep
and all the glory that fills the darkness of night

Allow me to paint on the canvas of your heart and imagine
the royalty of His majestic nights and the splendor of the
beauty it unveils that of our Heavenly Father. The Creator
of the universe has gifted our eyes to behold and our
minds to become fascinated, by our hearts. Intrigued by
it as I sat looking out of my window on the sixth floor

I thought I'd look upward to catch a glimpse of His
magnificent glory that unfolds during the night

As I gazed upward hoping to see the stars
twinkling in all its shining light

I discovered the splendor of the night

No trafficking of people moving about could I see

The cars that once fled up and down the streets were
halted and had come to almost a complete stand still

The City appeared to be resting

As the night grew old the waves that once was tossing
and slapping to and fro were now silent and still

It appeared to be a sleepy blue ocean

And Oh' what a blessing

"How Splendid Is The Night" *(continued)*

He had calmed the wind and the storms and
the rains that had fallen so heavily

The cold air ceased and the night grew on.

The crispness of the air had settled like a charm

The sidewalk during the day that produces harm in some way
was now safe for night was quiet and all appeared asleep

As I beheld such a royal view of nature in
all its splendor fresh and anew

I realized it was the Master's touch that created this wondrous view

No painter can capture all the beauty of the night

It speaks to the heart with all its charms that's just right

Way up high above the earth there's a
hidden part of this whole world

It only comes to life at night

It causes all the senses to be awaken, it shakes
and stirs one pure imagination

The heart is awed by the magnificent color of midnight blue

The glory of clouds no longer in view

The sky scrolls back and its like a naked floor you see

Its this amazing midnight blue that goes as far as the eye can see

The moon is suspended hanging in space giving
off light by God's amazing grace

Its the silence of the night that captivates the
mind and brings an unforgettable thrill

There is a peace, a tranquility if you will, like none other found here

Such a peaceful place of solitude one can only
embrace it as the senses awakens

Such heavenly bliss is hard to resist

"How Splendid Is The Night" *(continued)*

The business of the day gone by, and just you yourself investing
in the night, for it is your right to have a peaceful good night

The trees outside my window are standing so
tall-shoulders are big and oh so broad

The grass is blooming stretching forth in the soil laid by
the gentle breeze from the dawning of the night

How breathtakingly beautiful it all appears.

One could sit back and relax, and forget about those terrible years

There's smiles and cheers in this atmosphere

No room for tears nor quandras that can produce fears

You see all is at rest for the night is near

Here the safety of His arms embraces you my
dear, to just be, just, be of good cheer

With this breathtaking view in mind

I salute my savior as I bid thee goodnight.

I bow at your feet with gratitude in heart and pray
I'll awake with a fresh view of you in sight

From My Heart to yours

for the splendor of this whole vast great
world. How awesome is this place....

The beauty of the night

To the watchman on the wall who keeps
the city while I sleep at night

All praise glory and honor to the most High God

Deborah Boone

"Creating My World"

Here in my world all the doors are shut to
all the chaos and noise without

Nothing can enter that can form without light

My world is bright and peaceful a place of solitude

The doors are always open where I can
come and sup with my Father

He's never weary of my hearing

He welcomes me with open arms

He knows I'm dependent and depending on Him

I'm privileged by God that He should speak to me so

For He opens up His treasure chest and pours out riches untold

There is a beauty here so rare no human mind can compare it

Nothing on earth can describe it

There is no beauty nowhere that is like it

Here in my world its exciting to be in the presence of the Almighty

The table is always spread with such delicacies

There is bread called manna sweet as can be

Its the words of His mouth deposited inside of me

The angels delight and share and take part

"Creating My World" *(continued)*

Here they await to hear the Master's heart

They go to and fro as messengers of God

Sharing His private thoughts to those both
near and far depositing to every heart

Have you ever been touched by the saviours love?

It transforms you beyond any human touch

His love is pure more precious than gold

As His eyes behold our needs here below

Such beauty can never be told

How sweet are the words that drop from His lips

Each one carefully thought of designed to fit

Whatever your need whatever your care He has mounds to share

Here there is no labor

Just beauty rare

A place of tranquility surrounded all with care

He's ever attentive to your every word

Never are you ever unheard

He eagerly awaits His time with you

You see He has a special place in His heart for you

If ever a tear should fall from your eyes

He takes His own hands and dry them away

Immediately a cup of joy is waiting to fill the place of your aching

He's thoughtful, He's caring, He's mindful for
His son, once walked in this world too

He shouldered His burdens and rolled them away

He re-created His world a brand new glorious day

Deborah Boone

"Creating My World" *(continued)*

Ahh this world I am creating a get away place
where there is rest and solitude

A place hidden in the heart where I can depart

From life's hustle and bustle

A place where I can come and be seated at His throne

Ahh this world I am creating a get away place
where there is rest and solitude

A place hidden in the heart where you can come too
and get away from life's hustle and bustle

A place where I can come and be seated at His throne

Ahh this world that I am creating

I've never seen the likes nowhere throughout His creation
that can touch this place hidden inside of me

There's beauty rare everywhere

The moment I spend with Him in His presence alone
causes my heart to rejoice and I am filled with ecstasy

I hear the words gently spoken to my heart they are embraced

And never is he far

He's always near just a prayer away

To fill every longing of the heart day after day

How gracious is He

How mindful, How thoughtful

How wonderful to know this my savior

To God be the glory for the wonder that He is

For the gracious love that He has imparted to all that will hear

God is love and He pours it out without measure

He sups with us He abides with us He loves to hear
us and He is always near ever present

"Creating My World" *(continued)*

There's a place in our hearts where we can go and
get in touch anytime of the day or night

There's a place we can go that abides in our innermost being

A reservoir He has poured in of the spirit of the Holy Ghost

He's a faithful companion, He's all that God is

He abides and lives inside of us

If ever we are without a friend

Knowing not which way to go, which way to turn

There's a place deep inside that will come alive

When we call and when we cry

He's ever present ever near His love He never minds giving it
out measurelessly Ahh, this my world I am creating everywhere
I look is brand new to me I see sights I've never seen

Dreams I dare to imagine I see beauty rare

I see through my struggles through my troubles the glory
unfolding, the mystery held at bay now released that through His
glory is His from all the suffering and through the years of toil

How great is His riches

How marvelous His mighty works

How awesome, is this! God words will never
describe feelings will never tell

There is no way, no way to express the love He has invested in us.

Some call Him a matchless wonder

Some call Him Jehovah, some call Him El Shaddai, The
Almighty God some call Him Creator of the World

He's all that and more. Whatever you call Him He is there with thee

Deborah Boone

"Creating My World" *(continued)*

Whatever your relationship with Him

He's Daddy, He's Papa, HE's Abba Father

Whatever your need He is there with thee

To Shiloh be the glory for all He has done in my life

Its such an honor to be with you O' Lord

"Friends"

Friends are a gift from God

They're rare, few in number some are chosen to be for a lifetime

Friends true friends will tell the real deal and keep on loving you

Sometimes most often a friend can be closer than a sister or brother

Real friends are a treasure

You can pour out your heart too

They'll listen attentively and in the end they'll offer
sound advice and give you the support you need

Yes! A real friend you won't find many in a lifetime

Friends are like a hidden treasure.

Full of secret riches they always have your best interest at heart

Friends have that special ability to stay bonded in hard times

Friends are special people they're some one you can
tell all your troubles to and can confide in

They're counselors, they're business consultants, partners, fun
to be with and offer the security of your safety in many ways

They're a precious gift to treasure from God if they are a true friend

"Home Is Where The Heart Is"

I know that I know that I'm going home

Was the sound that cried deep inside the heart

Its a place where I belong wrapped in your arms,

free from all harm,

Where I can feel the comfort of your love

And the security I do know where I can
lay my head upon your breast

And rest, rest, rest

I'm coming home to the place where I belong

A place prepared to receive me as your own

I'm coming home where I can wrap up in your arms and
feel the comfort of your love deep down inside of me

A place I long to be where I'm free free free

I'm coming home, where I can have the peace I
need because of the strength I find in you.

I know that I'm going home we've been apart far to
long and our hearts are crying out come home

No longer apart do I wish to be

I want to see you, hear you know that you're near

"Home Is Where The Heart Is" *(continued)*

I want to curl up beside you and tell you just how dear you are to me

So Honey, I know I'm coming home that's where I long to be.

A place that's prepared to receive me as your own

Where I can sleep at night and bid thee good night

Awake the next day and behold your smiling face

I just want to be with you to just start our lives anew

Deborah Boone

"I'm Blessed"

I'm blessed, I'm blessed, I'm blessed

I have a treasure Oh so rare

It's priceless

To me none can compare

I have a treasure, called Essence Rare

A lifetime to treasure you see we're a pair

He's the love of my life

He chose me for His wife

Honored in deed am I to be His

Women dream of a Knight in Shining Armour

They even boast that their man is the best of most

But, I dare to say to all who wait

Seek God's face and just wait

For the priceless jewel He has given me
has been worth every heartache

Through the storms, through the rains, through fire, I came

But in the end it was worth waiting for

I was tested, I was tried but God said in Him (Jesus)

"I'm Blessed" *(continued)*

He found my heart to be pure gold

He said my daughter

You've proven to me to be one of my best

So out of my hidden treasure chest I've
reserved for you my very best

He's faithful you see, He only has eyes for me

His love is unwavering although he has had
to endure many a hard trying times

He's adorable you see, and I can't help but
smile from deep down inside of me

Oh what a man and I'll love him till the end

He's tall, He's bold, He does not shatter in front of any foe

He has a mind all his own

Yet He's kind, He's my love song

He's strong, one that commands respect when you see him

He's confident, sharp, keen eyed and watchful

You see He listens from His heart

He's a fine work of art

He has a heart that touches you from deep within

You can't help but marvel

He's my best friend

I admire Him, He is my inspiration

He's one of a kind, and He's mine all mine

He's my joy, no matter what unhappiness unfolds in a day

He's my strength when I'm awake

He's carried in my heart so I'm assured we won't depart

Deborah Boone

"I'm Blessed" (continued)

He's faithful to his word a man I know I can trust

He's someone you just want to be with, never grow tired of

He causes me to dream

He's the beauty of every awakening day

He's my cozy comfort every sleeping night

He's my sunshine in the midst of my rainy day

He's my King I sit upon a pedestal way up high
in my heart. I do honor and respect him.

You see He is my five star general in the army of the Lord

He's my comforter and I love just being in His arms.

He's the wind beneath my feet for He speaks
and my heart seeks to fulfill His desires

He's my life He's the best of my world for He indeed is my world

I know no other place. I'd rather be on this side of heaven.

Then to be seated in His presence I have a jewel, Essence Rare

He's quite a man and my father in heaven says He has given me
the best of the best now go on in life but take care of my son,

I've chosen for you

For I reached into my treasure chest because
I loved you through such great tests.

You stood for me and I'm honoring you with my very best
my son whom I've set my honor and favor upon.

For I have found Him worthy and have set my
seal of approval upon the 2 of you.